ALAN MACFARLANE was born in Shillong, India, in 1941 and educated at the Dragon School, Sedbergh School, Oxford and London Universities. He is the author of over twenty published books, including *The Origins of English Individualism* (1978) and *Letters to Lily: On How the World Works* (2005). He has worked in England, Nepal, Japan and China as both an historian and anthropologist.

He was elected to the British Academy in 1986 and is now Emeritus Professor of Anthropology at the University of Cambridge and a Life Fellow of King's College, Cambridge.

How To Understand Each Other
Notes for Nina

ALAN MACFARLANE

2018

CAM RIVERS PUBLISHING

First published in Great Britain in 2018

5 Canterbury Close
Cambridge CB4 3QQ

www.cambridgerivers.com
press@cambridgerivers.com

Author: Alan Macfarlane
Series Editor: Zilan Wang
Editor: Sarah Harrison
Marketing Manager: James O'Sullivan
Typesetting and cover design: Jaimie Norman

The publication of this book has been supported by
the Kaifeng Foundation.

For Nina Turin, with my love

Alan Macfarlane, 2017

Map of Civilizations

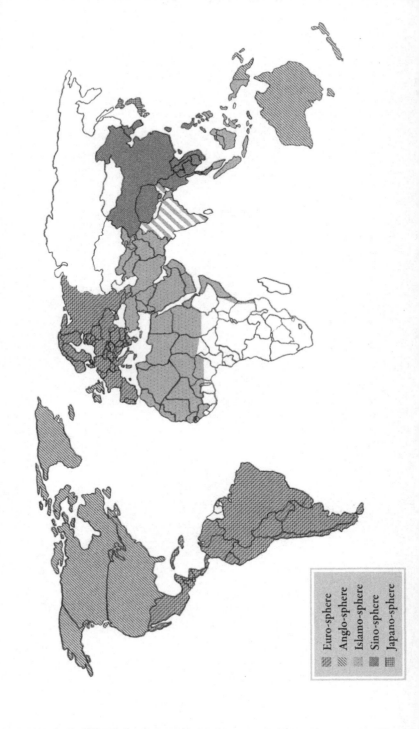

Euro-sphere
Anglo-sphere
Islamo-sphere
Sino-sphere
Japano-sphere

Contents

Why I Am Writing to You

D^{EAR} NINA,

You live in a great multicultural city in Canada, where you meet people from different civilisations, including the descendants of the first peoples of the American continent, who migrated over from Asia tens of thousands of years ago. You must sometimes wonder about the origins and nature of the civilisations which produced the Chinese, Japanese, Indians and Europeans you encounter. And already you have travelled several times to the very different civilisation of Nepal in the Himalayas and met people whose lives are so far removed from yours. So this book is for you as someone growing up in a world which is so far away from that in which I was a young person in the middle of the twentieth century.

My childhood world only had about two and a half billion inhabitants. Yours now has almost seven and a half billion and by the time you are my age may well have at least double that. So it is already a much more crowded world and will become more so.

Your world sees huge flows of people travelling from country to country – to find jobs, to be educated, to have holidays, or to find safety from danger and death. So you meet people from all over the world as your neighbours and school friends.

When I was a child it took over a month for a letter to my parents in India to reach them and for them to reply to me. I hardly ever saw any news or pictures of most of the world in my early childhood except in geography lessons. China, India, Africa hardly entered into my school life and I very seldom met people from these places.

Your world has immediate electronic contacts with all of the planet. With your cellphone, iPad, Internet, television, social media links, you can potentially travel anywhere and learn about almost anything. You can make friends with people anywhere in the planet and talk to them on Skype, or write to them freely by email or Twitter. You are digitally connected in a way which I could not have dreamt of as a child.

Even when I went to University at Oxford I did not study the history or current life of anyone outside Britain in my course except for one paper on western Europe in the Middle Ages. I knew practically nothing about world history or the cultures and customs of the nine tenths of the world's population outside Europe and America.

All that is changed and you are now becoming a world citizen. I hope that, like your Mum and Dad, you will travel and study across the planet. I hope that you will become ever more interested in the global problems that face us all – poverty, population pressures, new diseases, women's rights, destruction of the environment, global warming, deep political differences. I hope that you will contribute to making our world a fairer and happier place.

If you are to prepare yourself to do this, and if you are to face the huge challenges of cultural mixing that we see around us, it is essential for you to understand others. Not just understanding on the surface – how your friends eat different foods, worship different gods, sing different songs – but much deeper, how our planet came to be occupied by so many varied peoples and civilisations; where they originated, how they are moving, and how they can continue in their inner essence and live together.

So I have written this little book for you, a citizen of the world, to try to pass on something of what I have learnt, in my long life as a historian and anthropologist, about human variety and human similarity. Many visits to different civilisations – different parts of Britain, Europe, Nepal and India, Japan, China, Australia and America and elsewhere, have made me think constantly about how these places work. The following is a small bit of what I have learnt.

Obviously this is a huge subject, for every country is different, and within each there are often vast variations. I hope you will be able to shade in the details of the picture from your experiences. Yet I thought it would be helpful to give you a first rough map of five of the world's great and ancient civilisations – China, Japan, the Islamo-sphere, Europe and the English-speaking peoples. When you have the shape of the wood you can invest investigate particular trees.

When I was in Burma recently I was taken up in a hot-air balloon to float over the more than a thousand temples and pagodas of Pagan (Bagan). Rising up through the mist as the sun broke and seeing the glories of those ancient red buildings, caught in a noose of light; drifting onwards, occasionally dropping to examine a particularly wonderful example, was an extraordinary experience. I hope you will one day share it.

This book is my attempt to lift you up above your everyday world in a Canadian city in order to drift across vast and ancient civilisations which have shaped you in so many ways. You will, I hope, see something of their complexity and yet simplicity, their beauty and their limitations.

One day I hope you will live in a world where the present struggles, shortages and confusions are reduced. That will only happen if we learn to understand rather than hate and dismiss, each other. In doing so, in understanding and appreciating others, you will understand yourself better.

You will come to realise that your roots are all over the world, not just your blood roots in Italy, Holland and Britain, but your deep intellectual and cultural roots all over Europe, Asia and the Americas. You are the sum and heir of all of human history. As such a 'global soul,' here is part of your world, drifting below you.

ONE

How Do We Understand Each Other?

He who understands the past,
understands the present.
He who understands the present,
may understand the future.

— ADAPTED FROM GEORGE ORWELL

T HE NEED FOR mutual understanding has never been greater. Yet the difficulty of achieving such an understanding has also never been more extreme. The two facts are linked. We live in a confused and confusing world which has thrown very different cultures and civilisations into close contact. Humans have encountered other peoples with different histories and lifestyles for thousands of years. Yet it is just in the last generation, less than thirty years, in which the process has been magnified hugely.

We know the reasons for this. There is much greater travel and there are new waves of migration and flight on a new scale. The explosive development of the media, from television to smartphones, now bring us contrasting images and values. The rapid changes of the computer and Internet revolution have created a global economy, society and to a certain extent politics – but one where the differences have not been ironed out.

The rushing changes in society and culture over a very short period of time mean that people have to absorb new ways of thinking and acting almost instantaneously. It is no wonder that many people, especially those living in the rapidly changing civilisations outside the West, feel a sense of vertigo – of falling through space with nothing to hold them to any fixed certainties.

What have I learned in my life as a historian and anthropologist which may make it easier for others to understand what is happening and to understand each other?

* * *

The task of both history and anthropology is to go beneath the surface of the present in order to understand the deeper patterns which have shaped human societies. The aim is to find a level where we can understand what generates daily events and explains the confusions we encounter. There are various ways of thinking about what this involves.

What we are trying to do is to understand the grammatical rules that create the language of culture. For example, what are the gender rules, the religious rules, the economic rules, the artistic rules which lie deep in a society or civilisation which permit it to exist over time? What are the deeper tendencies which, if we understand, will explain what we observe in individual lives and thoughts?

If we think of this in relation to music, we are trying to understand what the Japanese thinker Maruyama Masao called the 'deep note' of a culture – what he also called the *basso ostinato* or reverberating but unchanging bass note. Maruyama thought he had discovered this for Japan and I shall explain what I have learned from him about that civilisation. Yet the metaphor can be extended to other cases. For example, what is the 'deep note' of China, the Islamo-sphere, Europe or the English-speaking world? How does this reverberating bass affect the higher notes through the course of time?

Anthropologists have devised their own methods to study the deeper levels or 'patterns' of culture. In the early days they tried to find the customs which shaped the world. They investigated the patterns of living as individuals, families and societies, the way people earned a living through hunting and agriculture, how they shaped their environment through crafts and technologies, and how they communicated through language and arts. All these were guided by largely unspoken and unwritten codes, which it was not easy for people in the societies in question to put into words. Yet people knew how to act and think because of them, having learnt them progressively from the moment of their birth. More recently this idea of generative customs has been rephrased by Pierre Bourdieu in his idea of 'habitus,' that is the un-articulated habits or dispositions which shape the way we think and act, without being fully conscious of them.

Another way of thinking about this is to use the analogy of a game. As we observe the five civilisations which I shall briefly analyse, we can see that each is playing a complicated game through time. Each of the games has a different set of rules, known by the players, which allows people to gain a living and an identity. The games are as different as cricket, football or tennis. Only if we understand the rules of each game will we start to appreciate and understand each other.

My final metaphor is from my garden. It is filled with many kinds of trees – apples, pears, cherries, silver birch, chestnut, oak, ginkgo. Each grows in its own way and with its own rules. Yet they coexist and thrive. They start as a tiny nut and end as huge, majestic and complex entities. So our task is to understand what is contained in the original seed and to watch how the branches and twigs and leaves unfurl over time and how each tree keeps its constantly evolving relations with other living things in the garden.

To penetrate to the heart, the essence, the deep structures of other cultures, whose history is unfamiliar, and whose rules are totally different from our own, is difficult. It requires an imaginative leap from our own familiar world into other worlds, a suspension of our prejudices and assumptions and a willingness to listen to other stories. Yet we all do this every time we read a book, watch a film, or meet a stranger. What we are doing is scaling up our human ability to enter other worlds through our imagination and empathy.

* * *

I have chosen these civilisations partly because I know four of them from personal experience. But I have left out another, Nepal, which I know very well, because I am concentrating on the most influential and powerful of world civilisations today. Their dealings with each other affects the rest of the world, as well as their own internal affairs.

There are some simple techniques which I have found useful in this scaling up and which I have applied to the analysis of the five civilisations briefly sketched below. One is the use of comparisons. We can never understand ourselves, let alone others, unless we are constantly comparing situations. Comparing does not mean just contrasting – 'they do this, we do the opposite.' It means looking to see what is in common as well as what is different. For example, the different nations of Europe have much in common – religion, language, law, history, art – yet are also very different in many ways. The same is true as between Europe and America, or Japan and China. Comparison makes the over-familiar in our own world strange and visible and it makes others, that are so strange that we cannot at first understand them, into something more comprehensible.

The second tool is to combine the past and the present. We cannot understand what now exists without looking into its history. In the case of the five civilisations in this book that means at least one thousand years or more, as we watch each civilisation grow like a tree. Yet equally we cannot understand each of them if we do not look at their present – watch the developments today and, if possible, spend time talking to people from that culture and visiting them for serious investigation. The more 'participant-observation' fieldwork we can do in another culture, the more chance is there that we shall penetrate deeper into its hidden worlds.

The third methodology, linked to the use of history, is to examine particularly closely what has been called the 'point of origin.' The first step, the first sentence, the first seed, the first trickle of a great river, has a very long and continuing influence on everything that happens afterwards. We shall see this in our case studies, where the different points of origin of Christianity and Islam, or of Japan and China, made these civilisations, though adjacent, very different from each other.

Another method is to treat cultures or civilisations as a whole, as packages, bundles, as orchestras or teams. We will not understand China, the Islamo-sphere or America if we just look at one part – economy, politics, society or language. Cultures and civilisations are composites of language, traditions, ideologies, geographies and much more. They have to be considered as we would consider a great painting or symphony. We would never appreciate the Mona Lisa or Beethoven's Fifth Symphony if we just concentrated on one corner of the painting or one instrument in the orchestra. All civilisations are total entities – and can only be understood as such.

Finally, and as a continuation of that idea, we can see that civilisations and cultures are bundles of relations. That is to say, it is not a particular thing, for example the family system, or the system of aesthetics, or the political system, that will reveal the nature of a civilisation. It is *the relations between* these spheres, for example the family and the economy, or the religion and the politics, or the art and the technology. So we need to watch how these relations change over time and we also need to study *the relations of relations*, for example how the relationship of man to woman is similar to the relation of day and night, sun and moon, ruler and ruled in China.

We now know what the aim of this small book is – to understand better our confused world and the peoples from different cultures and civilisations we are increasingly interacting with. In order to do this, we need to probe the hidden grammars, melodies, rules and customs. We have five simple methods to help us approach such an understanding. The last thing to specify is the object of our analysis – what are the units or entities which can best help us to understand our extraordinary, complex and rapidly changing world?

* * *

For most of human history and for most people, when people lived in small bands or tribes, the only other humans you needed to understand were those you encountered face-to-face, from your own and neighbouring communities. Later, as civilisations emerged, if you were a trader or a soldier, you might encounter complete strangers with different religions and traditions. Yet normally you learnt from childhood how to understand your family, village and region, comprising a few thousand people.

The number and diversity of those whom people encountered increased greatly with the rise of empires and then of nationstates, particularly from the nineteenth century. As a British or Dutch imperialist, or French or Russian politician or intellectual, you would need to understand people who spoke different languages and obeyed different customs to yourself. Particularly among the ruling class at the centre of large European Empires, there was a good deal of knowledge of the rest of the world, and European curiosity about the world was stimulated by the great voyages and trade links from the sixteenth century.

Yet until the 1980s, this wider awareness, as I remember from my own upbringing, applied to only a few people from other civilisations. Most people living in America, or China or Turkey until recently did not need to understand much about people from very different cultures and civilisations. Almost all those you met, read about in your papers or even watched on your television screens, were rather like you. Maybe they were of a different class and education and perhaps even religion, but you felt an imagined community with them. They were, like you – French, Italian, American, Japanese.

The extraordinary communications revolution, expansion of world trade, migration waves, educational exchanges of the last thirty years means that many people now have a need to understand worlds far from their own personal experience. This little book will try to provide some guidance in such a situation.

* * *

So what is the most effective unit to understand our current situation? What we need is the largest and widest unit in which people shape their identity, share a common history and culture, so that they feel in some sense 'We.' This used to be the village, then the tribe, then the nation-state. It is now a civilisation. We can sense this when we come to study the five civilisations dealt with below – China, Japan, the Islamo-sphere, Europe and the English speaking world.

Like love, beauty or fear, it is impossible to define a civilisation - but we know it when we encounter it. A civilisation can be thought of appropriately not just as a geographical and physical entity, lines on a map, but as an imagined and constructed entity which stretches far beyond the borders on that map. This stretching outside the conventional limits of a physical location is indeed behind much of the feeling that we live in a globally integrated, yet at times confrontational, world.

I have used the suffix 'sphere' to try and capture the idea that they are no longer geographically located entities. I first encountered the idea of sphere, previously used in the Cold War in relation to 'spheres of influence,' in relation to my own civilisation. James Bennett and others termed this the 'Anglo-sphere,' to make it possible to encompass not only Britain and America but also places like Canada, Australia and even to a certain extent India and other parts of the former British Empire.

Using this idea, one can see that the 'Sino-sphere' now spreads over all of eastern Asia and even to a considerable extent into Europe, the Americas and even Africa. The Islamo-sphere stretches over the vast traditional area of Islamic civilisations but also beyond that to Europe, America, China and elsewhere. The Euro-sphere covers all of western and eastern Europe to the Ural mountains, and South America and many parts of the former Continental Empires. In a virtual way, through its technology, economy and the arts, the Japano-sphere stretches way beyond the islands of Japan.

If we are going to understand each other we need to recognise these civilisational entities, which are like tectonic plates – massive, slowly moving, buckling, bending and building. They are each very different, yet they have to co-exist in peace, otherwise we are in danger of destroying ourselves as a species.

So I will first briefly describe five of these spheres of influence, four of which (Anglo, Euro, Sino, Japan) I know from personal experience and the fifth (Islam) through reading. At the end I will try to suggest briefly how, rather than a 'clash of civilisations,' they could, and must, live in harmony.

TWO

The Sino-sphere

C HINA IS THE oldest surviving civilisation on Earth, with roots going back over five thousand years and united into one empire 2200 years ago. Within China today live a fifth of the human species, and at times in the past up to one third of the human population of the planet lived in China. Its land-mass is equivalent to all of Western and Eastern Europe and parts of North Africa and the Middle East.

The Chinese invented many of the great technologies – the compass, clocks, gunpowder, printing, silk, paper, tea and porcelain. Its past greatness is being retrieved and it is likely to again become the most powerful economic, political and cultural power on earth within the next generation. Only in the last few centuries of its 2200 year history has it not been so. All our lives are being, and will be, hugely shaped by China.

Yet very few people outside China, even in Japan, let alone in the West, have much understanding of this great civilisation. At first sight, coming to terms with its immensity looks daunting.

China is hugely diverse geographically and ecologically, from the snowy north to the tropical south, from the Himalayas in the west to the Pacific in the east. It is culturally diverse with a hundred million minority peoples alongside the 1.3 billion Han Chinese. The peoples of China speak many different languages and have widely different customs and histories. Its majestic and recorded history encompasses great events from before well before Confucius and his fellow philosophers two and a half thousand years ago, through the glories of the Tang, Sung and Ming up to the present. It has suffered great invasions and changes caused by the Mongols, the Manchus, the Western Powers and the Japanese. To generalise about it seems impossible.

Yet I think that a number of simple keys will give us a way of understanding how this great civilisation survived intact and how a vast population and landmass is held together. Understanding this will help us to see how China has and will shape our world.

* * *

The first feature is language. China, as well as the neighbouring countries which have adopted the Chinese characters, is extraordinary in being the only great civilisation on Earth which has retained a fully non-alphabetical written language. This written script holds China together, containing thousands of characters, each one the equivalent of one or several words in an alphabetical script. Hence it is called a logographic script (logos meaning a word). Each character is also a picture, hence it is sometimes called a pictographic language. Most Chinese children, and many Koreans, Japanese and others throughout the centuries have had to learn the simple form of this written language.

This means that at a certain level all the millions of Chinese can communicate over vast differences of culture and local tradition. The language is central to the identity of the Chinese and through its extraordinary combination of a meaning which lies both in the shape of the character and the character itself, it combines two elements which have been separated in alphabetical systems. Chinese writing is both painting and writing in the Western sense. Calligraphy is a great art which bridges the divide between the eye and the ear.

The amazing writing system is associated with the vast literature of China, a huge tradition of all kinds of writing, from philosophy to history, from novels to poetry. China is the greatest literary civilisation in history and also the most educated. It is this educational system which also provides a key to understanding China.

* * *

From at least two thousand years ago, after the destruction of the traditional feudal system, China developed a unique combination of education and bureaucracy. Anticipating the West by two thousand years, the Chinese instituted a comprehensive system of education stretching all over the empire. At the bottom was a widespread primary education, for a year or two and in order to learn a basic set of characters.

On top of this there was a graded set of schools. Students moved through these levels by passing competitive examinations. The successful moved up from level to level until those who were most brilliant at the kinds of memory and analytical work required, were promoted as senior bureaucrats all over China with the most able in the Emperor's court.

There was no separate class of a large military nobility, no educated set of churchmen, no parliament selected by wealthy voters, to rule China. Instead there was an immense bureaucratic pyramid, through which, in theory, the poorest boy, in the most remote child had an outside chance of one day becoming a powerful mandarin. It was the original meritocratic state.

The whole vast empire was run by a highly trained and expert, civilian, bureaucracy. The mandarins were moved constantly to prevent corruption and they acted as administrators and judges. Nowhere else in the world has such a system been tried out until very recently. It appears extremely modern, despite its ancient roots in the Qin unification of China and taken on by the Han in the early part of the Christian Era.

The political-bureaucratic system is a key to China's unity and durability. It is a vast and complex set of allegiances and sub-allegiances, with each person or official owing loyalty to the level above. A village headman was responsible to the local sub-provincial official, the province to the region, and all the regions to the Emperor and his court. This was the only way in which hundreds of millions of people could be united politically into a nation state.

It means that today provinces the size of a large European country, some of them individually with the wealth of India or Russia are held together in a complex federation, a federation over four times the population size of the United States.

* * *

The strength of this integration was increased by blending it with the enduring and central features of its great philosophical age. Confucius, Mencius, Laotze and the earlier Legalists, working approximately two and a half thousand years ago, devised a system which is widely known as 'Confucianism.' This is at heart an ethical and social philosophy. It teaches that every person owes respect, and is linked to, those above and below him or her.

At the lowest level this is largely within the realms of the family. Above all there is the duty to respect and obey a father, and this is extended to the relations between husband and wife, younger brother and older brother and so on throughout the family and clan, junior respecting senior members. This system then extends back through the generations to grandparents and even to the dead ancestors in their tombs and halls.

This obligation is enshrined in the law codes of the Tang, Sung, Ming, Qing and even up to the present. Duty, respect, loyalty, consideration, support, mutual understanding and harmony, all these are the basis of morality and identity and they apply not just to one's family but also to the state. The relations you have with your father are a parallel chain to your relations with your political superiors, and particularly the Emperor. So the social and political worlds are fused, there is no separation. This is one of the most important keys to Chinese strength. Yet it also has immense consequences for its ability to absorb other political and social systems.

* * *

It may be wondered where religion comes into all of this. In much of the rest of the world, and even in large areas of western China with Muslims in the north-west and the Buddhists of Tibet, Mongolia and adjacent provinces, religion is very important. The extraordinary fact is that to a large extent religion, as we understand it in the West, is a minor feature of most of Chinese history.

There are many local folk beliefs, cults, ancestor worship, and rituals. Yet religion, at a civilisational level and as a central feature of the identity and integration of China, is largely absent. Confucius and Mencius were not interested in religion. Taoism is a nature cult with no single God. Buddhism is of course not really a religion since there is no God, and in any case was systematically downplayed through much of Chinese history. Buddhism was not absorbed in the central institutions of power. The Emperor may be given his 'mandate' by 'Heaven,' but heaven is very vague indeed.

The relative absence of religiosity and of the idea that 'religion,' of the kind found in the monotheistic West, is absent, has meant that China never had any of the religious wars of the kind that we find through the history of Islam and Christianity. It is possible to be simultaneously a Buddhist, Confucian, Daoist and perhaps even a Christian or Muslim to a certain extent.

Though there were massive millenarian (end of the world) uprisings from time to time – for example the White Lotus, the Taiping and the Boxer, when at least seventy million, and perhaps over twice that number, died, these were religious movements *against* the imperial powers, or against foreigners. These horrific events have made successive Chinese governments extremely nervous about any kind of quasi-religious movements. The threat of disturbances which can sweep across China and cause vast numbers of deaths helps to explain the apparent over-reactions to the Dalai Lama, the Falun Gong and any kind of attempt to introduce political religion, and to take over the government through rebellion.

* * *

The absence of religion also explains the absence of another feature which we find in the two Western monotheisms – Islam and Christianity – namely proselytising crusades. There is no central religious identity to be spread in China or by the Chinese Empire abroad. You can become Chinese (Han) by living like a Han – your food, clothes, language, family customs define you as such. It is a style of living rather than a religious identity. You do not have to believe something about the existence of a particular God.

So while from time to time the Chinese emperors made great expeditions to subdue or push back neighbouring powers – Korea, Japan, Vietnam, Burma, the central Asiatic sultanates – this was done for political and sometimes economic reasons. It was undertaken to prevent incursions into China, exact tribute, and open up new land and trade for the expanding Han.

This explains why China hardly ever pursued the dream of overseas imperial expansion. Apart from two attempts by the Mongol rulers in the thirteenth century to invade Japan, and another to try to invade Indonesia, it never used its navies to try to seize other lands. Its huge ships could have founded an overseas empire in the fifteenth century when they voyaged as far as East Africa. They took gifts, trade goods, and greetings rather than guns and religious texts on their several voyages. They never attacked or settled in the lands which they discovered.

This points to a different model of State and Empire to that in the West. We need to think of China, the Middle Kingdom, as the sun, with its tributary states like planets circling around it – Korea, Japan, Vietnam, Tibet. They were thought of as distant family, living away in new lands, owing respect and acknowledging links, but independent and not part of the Middle Kingdom itself. It is misleading to apply Western ideas of either the way in which the British Empire, for example, worked in relation to India or Canada, or the way in which nation states existed in the West from the eighteenth century. We are dealing with a unique 'civilisational state' which is structurally different from anything in western experience. We can learn a great deal from it.

I am also struck by the degree to which the Confucian emphasis on harmony, balance, mutual tolerance and respect, and the rational sorting out of differences, is central to the long Chinese history. This will come out more clearly when we contrast it with the central characteristics of three civilisations further to the West – the Islamo-sphere, Europe and the Anglo-sphere. The philosophy and political sciences, the political and legal systems, and even the games of the more western civilisations are based on an adversarial and competitive idea of 'the survival of the fittest' which is very different from the Chinese tradition.

* * *

It has been suggested that most civilisations are held together by a division of labour or function in the society. An example of this is the four interlocking orders or *varna* as they are called in India. This four-fold functional classification stretches across much of the Indo-European world, from the Indian caste system to the social orders which predominated through most of European history.

There were the fighters and rulers (nobility), the townsmen, traders and manufacturers (bourgeoisie), the religious specialists, scribes and administrators (priests and clerical class), and the mass of workers in the countryside (peasants). Each depended on the others. Each social order was like a part or organ of the body – head, stomach, arms and legs. Each depended on the other. It was, in Emile Durkheim's phrase, an 'organic solidarity.'

China has seldom been like this during the last two thousand years. The cities were never independent and strong and there was no separate 'bourgeoisie' of large manufacturers and traders. There was seldom any independent religious class or clergy. There was no institutionally separate military nobility based on fighting skills, forming a caste of warrior rulers. In China there were only the mandarins and literati on one side (rulers) and the rest of the population, composed of numerous small traders, manufacturers and a vast rural population of farmers. So China could not be held together by organic solidarity.

Instead China was unified along the chains of the family and the political and bureaucratic organisation, and by interpersonal ties. This Durkheim described as 'mechanical solidarity' because it is like identical parts in a machine, two cogs for example, side by side. Another model Durkheim used was of an earthworm, where each segment is a complete unit. You can chop a worm into bits and each bit will grow again, whereas if you chop off an animal's head, the rest cannot function. It is this mechanical solidarity which has made it possible for China to be shattered by catastrophic events such as the Mongol invasion, or the thirty years of Communist rule under Mao, and yet to revert quite quickly to its previous state

China is based on interpersonal ties, a vast network of.

one-to-one links, friends of friends. One expression of this is in the system of *guanxi*, meaning 'connections.' It is whom you know that has always been important outside the family. Each Chinese, particularly nowadays with higher mobility and small families, has to develop a set of complex, often hierarchical, links with other Chinese.

* * *

These are just a few of the features which strike me as a Western observer looking at China and it's a long history. There is the general absence of monotheistic religion; the absence of confrontational personal relations; the absence of imperialistic overseas adventuring; the handing over of most of the trading opportunities to non-Han (and hence the absence of understanding of other cultures); the absence of professional groups and of civil society associations above the level of the clan; the absence of a complex legal system where process is simple, there is little civil law, and punishment is harsh. On the other hand there is a huge interest in arts and literature; a huge respect for education as the main channel for mobility; vast energy; widespread loyalty and trustworthiness; toughness and ability to work with others.

The obvious question for us is how a civilisation which is in many ways based on premises so different from the West will change and adapt itself to fit with other traditions, and how far should it do so. In reverse, we are faced with the question of how far we also have to adapt.

In some ways the situation looks like oil and water. The individualistic, confrontational, capitalist, democratic, industrial, scientific, nationalistic, bellicose, highly religious West, which crashed into China in the nineteenth century and destroyed the last Empire, is again crashing into China today.

Yet it is now confronting a China which, unlike the nineteenth and early twentieth century, has learned how to use the new technologies, tools and market mechanisms, so that it is too powerful to be crushed again.

What seems clear is that China is like its national tree, ginkgo (which is the only survivor of a treelike plant from the age of the dinosaurs). The ginkgo is immensely tough and has many ways of spreading itself. The ginkgo survived the ice age and the atom bomb at Hiroshima. The Mongols failed to destroy China, as did the Manchus, the Western Powers and the Japanese.

On the surface, if you visit Shanghai, Beijing or any other of its great cities, China seems like a gleaming new civilisation with extraordinary dynamism. It has some of the best schools, hospitals and factories in the world. Yet behind all this there is the old China, based on human relations, attentive to social ethics, highly sophisticated and educated, hard-working and collaborative.

China has already lifted a tenth of humanity, some seven hundred million of its own citizens, out of poverty in the last thirty years. It is potentially raising millions more in Africa and elsewhere. It went through a massive urban and industrial revolution, on a scale and speed which was ten times greater than that in Britain, with less chaos, misery and pollution than in the British case. It remains in many ways, despite its defects, the most extraordinary and estimable of all civilisations.

THREE

The Japano-sphere

ALTHOUGH JAPAN IS relatively small, less than a tenth of the size of the population of China or the Islamo-sphere, it is worth investigating. Japan shows how a civilisation which is only separated by a few miles of sea from another great civilisation, China, can nevertheless, with a different point of origin and a stubborn resistance to being changed, be totally different from its neighbour. It retained, through well over a thousand years, an alternative kind of civilisation, not only to China and Korea, but to any other on earth.

This unique civilisation is also interesting because it somehow managed to adopt and adapt to Western scientific industrialism nearly three quarters of a century before any other society outside Europe and America. In doing so it retained its own 'Japanese-ness' while being a hugely successful economic power and, for a while, a highly aggressive and military one too. So it may have lessons for those facing the problem of combining the West and the East.

Above all Japan is interesting in itself. It is filled with deep contradictions, seeming to work by laws that are totally unfamiliar to anyone from outside, not just westerners, but the Chinese and its other neighbours. It centres its civilisation on the celebration of beauty and interpersonal closeness in a more extreme form than any other of our examples. So what is the generative grammar of Japan?

* * *

Japan consists of a series of narrow, rocky, volcanic, islands stretching from the frozen north to the tropical south and surrounded by a dangerous sea. It is close enough to Korea and China to be able to absorb advanced ideas and technologies. Yet it is far enough away, and protected enough, so that it can filter each of the incoming waves and reject what it does not want. So it derived the core of its written logographic characters – *kanji* – from China, but modified it hugely by adding two alphabets, *hiragana* and *kitegana*.

Nor did Japan abandon its own spoken language. The language is deeply puzzling, both in its origins and because it has almost no resemblance to any other. It is immensely fluid, with little use of tenses, personal pronouns, negative and positive and with words each of which has a diverse range of meanings. As a Japanese proverb puts it, 'language is a barrier to communication.' Silence, or communicating through the invisible speech of the stomach (*Haragei*)is the best form of interpersonal exchange.

As well as the written language, many of the Japanese arts and crafts were originally imported from Korea, China and elsewhere. This applies to porcelain and pottery, silk and paper, music and many of the visual arts, and the crafts of agriculture and manufacture. Yet in each case a high technology was reshaped as it came to Japan and often improved, or at least elaborated. For example, the steel swords were modelled on

Chinese manufacture, but the Japanese by the thirteenth century made swords of a quality higher than those anywhere else in the world. While the tea ceremony came from the mainland, the Japanese adapted into a far more elaborate and complex a version than that in China or Korea.

* * *

The same happened to the philosophies and religions which flowed from the continent. The Japanese imported Confucianism in several waves, firstly in the seventh to eighth centuries in the first period of Chinese influence, and then again in the neo-Confucianism of the eighteenth century. Thus the Japanese adopted the idea of ethical relations, harmony, respect for elders, and to a certain extent the superiority of the male sex. They absorbed the central idea of unequal relations between superior and inferior, what Chie Nakane has called the 'Vertical Society.'

Yet the Japanese also altered the central tenet of Confucianism, thus reshaping its whole philosophy. In China, loyalty to the Emperor and your father were synonymous. But if it came to a choice, to obey father or the Emperor if they disagree, the father came first. In Japan, this was reversed. The Emperor and the political powers were dominant. In other words, politics and the nation is stronger than family ties and sentiments. This is a dramatic shift.

It gives hints of a deeply different political and social order. The Chinese were held together by a civil bureaucracy, recruited through Confucian education, with no balance to the absolute authority of the Emperor. The Japanese briefly tried such an imperial system during the seventh to tenth centuries, but in the medieval period they reverted to a true feudal system.

This involved a split rule between two distinct rulers, the military leader or Shogun and the ritual and symbolic ruler, the Emperor. They were usually located in different cities and often in tension with each other. From this divided centre, only reunited after the overthrow of the Shogunate at the Meiji imperial restoration in 1868, there was a feudal devolution of power.

There were the great lords, the daimyo, with their castles and armies, who were granted whole provinces in return for loyalty to the centre. They were required to spend half their lives in the central court, and when they were not there to leave close family as guarantees of their loyalty. They in turn were supported by an armed minor gentry, the samurai or *bushi*, equivalent to the knights of the West. These armed samurai were granted smaller landholdings which they in turn granted out to families and communities, in return for rent and support.

This system of power, the one case of authentic centralised feudalism outside Western Europe, makes Japan almost identical to England over much of its recent history in terms of its feudal structure. Yet it is also different. Though the cities of Japan, like those of England, were powerful and to a considerable extent independent, and though there were the class of the equivalent of a minor gentry in the countryside, there never arose the institution of an elected parliament, consisting of representatives of the rich merchants and independent farmers which arose in England. So Japan was the closest civilisation to the Western political system, but also diverged greatly.

The basis of the political system was thus the contractual

ties of loyalty and service in return for delegated power. This gave rise to the central ethic of a gentlemanly code of honour – *bushi-do* – which is in many respects similar to that of the British gentleman. This included a code where your 'word is your bond,' and honesty, service, independence, all-round competence both in administration and in physical sports and war were the goals.

* * *

Furthermore, the feudal emphasis on contractual, agreed, delegation of power is linked to a curious similarity between the family system of Japan and England. China's family system was immensely powerful, based on blood ties through males, the equal and shared ownership of property by parents and children, controlled marriage, no adoption except of blood relatives, and hence large and powerful clans. The family and clan underpinned Chinese history and created a world where ultimately family relations are the bedrock of society. Almost all of law, economics, contact with the ancestors, political allegiances are generated by family ties through most of Chinese history.

The Japanese never adopted such a system. Instead, like the Anglo-Saxons, they trace their blood links through both males and females and they use a kinship terminology which isolated out the close family of parents and children. Uniquely outside England, they left almost all of their property to one child, or to a non-relative. This created a very individualistic, and in some ways highly uncertain and anxiety-inducing, family system.

In England no child could be certain of an inheritance, for parents could use a written will to leave all of their property either to one child, or even to a stranger. The feudal system required the holding together of the larger estates and emphasised single heir inheritance. This was usually the oldest male, or primogeniture, but it could be another.

The same impartible inheritance occurred in Japan, but was achieved not through written wills but through adoption. Unlike both China and England, adoption of non-kin was permissible and very frequent. So the link between the family (society) and the economy was broken in both England and Japan, but in different ways.

Such adoption occurred not just in relation to land and houses, but with almost all resources. Thus, even to this day, important artists (*kabuki* or painters), or *sumo* wrestlers, or even university academics, will name someone as their heir, 'adopt' them to succeed. This ensures that the best person, rather than an inadequate child, is chosen for the job.

In Japan this creates a highly contractual, efficient, yet familistic society. Much of business in Japan, from the small firms up to the great corporations which have continued over the last several hundred years, has the feeling of a family. Once recruited or 'adopted,' you are part of that 'family' – with lifetime guaranteed employment, until recently, and a total commitment, which means it is much more than just a job.

* * *

This leads us to another paradox in Japan. Each Japanese is very separate, for he or she may be ejected from his family in favour of others. The metaphor is of a single lobster in a lobster pot, attached by a rope to the other lobster pots – deeply alone. Yet at the same time, Japan has a sticky or embedded and deeply intertwined feeling. It has been described in another metaphor as a *natto* society, *natto* being fermented bean curd, the tendrils of which intertwine in an inseparable mass.

No Japanese has a unique meaning except in relation to others – there is no sound if only one hand claps. Each Japanese is under huge pressure to conform and to meet the expectations of others. This accounts for the extraordinary bravery, group effort and effectiveness of the Japanese in many of their activities, yet it also accounts for their well-known xenophobia.

Strangers are regarded with suspicion and it is difficult for an outsider to be absorbed. Even those Japanese who have lived abroad for a few years (who used to be killed if they returned) when they come back are held at arm's length. To be Japanese is not just a question of eating sushi, wearing a kimono on the right occasion, speaking the language fluently, bowing with the appropriate bend of the back according to relative status, going to shrines, even being born of Japanese parents. True Japanese-ness is shown in thousands of tiny signs and symbols which, if they are missing or become out of date, indicate that they have become strangers in Japan.

* * *

Equally minute attention is paid to daily living. Every scrap of dirt should be cleaned away in the house, the streets and even in the subways. Dirt, or 'matter out of place,' both real and symbolic, is threatening and there is a deep concern not to allow pollution, either of Japanese identity or of personal living.

Yet while there is a puritanical streak, there is, as is so often in Japan, also the opposite. There is a concept of the body and all of its needs, in particular in relation to sex, which strikes many observers as far from puritanical. The body, naked or clothed, was to be served and there was no great difference between eating and sex. The pornography, and the disastrous misunderstanding when the Japanese took their attitudes to China and Korea, are well known.

'Both/and' is central to everything one says about Japan. It is possible to argue that it is the most puritanical, or the most lascivious, the most artistic or the most insensitive, the most peaceful, or the most warlike, the most individualistic or the most group based, the most equal or the most hierarchical, the most capitalist or the most anti-capitalist. The contradictions, from an outsider's point of view, never end and they take us to the heart of exploring the Japanese mystery.

* * *

A visitor to Japan – the cities, towns and private homes – will be struck by how 'religious' Japan appears. There are numerous temples and shrines, processions and frequent public rituals, every *sumo* wrestling match or building site has its Shinto symbols. Many houses have a *butsidan* or ancestor-commemorating shrine. The mixture of Shinto (the nature religion, similar to Chinese Daoism), Buddhism and Confucianism seem to make Japan very religious.

Yet when you talk to the Japanese, you soon discover it is a society filled with ritualistic performances, but no 'Religion' in the Western sense. There is no word for 'Religion' in Japanese. Teenage schoolchildren whom I questioned had never heard of the Buddha, Confucius, Christ or God. Shinto has no God, Buddhism has no God and in the extreme reinterpretations of the new Buddhist sects of Japan, for example Zen, there is 'nothing.' In the same way, there is nothing in the most important Shinto shrine at Ise, except a mirror. Confucianism is a social philosophy and not a religion. So Japan is the most, and the least, religious of societies.

* * *

When we realise this, we suddenly see that beneath the surface, or behind the looking-glass (mirror) which Japan presents to everyone from outside, there is another world. We see ourselves not Japan, unless we have the good fortune to enter through that glass.

It is not just that things are reversed in Japan, as many visitors noticed, or that there are endless contradictions according to our way of thinking, but that the basic grammar is different. Maruyama's 'deep note' or *basso ostinato* is totally different in Japan from that of any other civilisation. It is an enduring continuity, hidden behind frequent and often considerable changes.

Japan looks ultramodern on the surface if you go round its amazing cities or travel on its incredible railways. Yet it is also ancient and continuous. In fact it is neither modern, pre-modern, or post-modern.

Japan is the one great civilisation which has not divided up its life into separate systems or institutions which we can call 'religion,' 'economy,' 'society' or 'polity.' It is as integrated and seamless as the shamanic world I discovered in Nepal. Yet it combines this integration with ruthless efficiency and enormous creativity.

Japan blends the ancient world, lost almost everywhere else, with the powerful technologies of the scientific and industrial revolution. It is a miracle and a marvel, immensely attractive yet somehow also disturbing. The filmmaker, Hayao Miyazaki, captured this strange combination in his films. Japan is just as odd as the world into which the little girl wandered in his 'Spirited Away.'

FOUR

The Islamo-sphere

THE KEY TO the Islamo-sphere lies in its point of origin; the place (Arabia), the time (early seventh century AD) and the nature of its founder, Muhammad. It was founded by a merchant who preached in opposition to the prevailing social and religious systems which had swirled around the Persian and Arabic world since the earliest civilisations. His prophetic vision was to destroy almost all that went before – strong kinship and other group loyalties, polytheistic religions, inequalities between rich and poor. These were to be replaced with a very simple, equal and universal faith.

This faith consisted in the total, contractual commitment to God or Allah and reverence for his prophet. Islam and Muslim literally mean total obedience, 'submission to the will of God.'

The new religion had little dogma or theology, it did not set up a separate church organisation with an ordained priesthood, bishops and cardinals, or monasteries. Islam consisted centrally of the command to obey the five pillars, that is to do, in your private way, five things. These were daily prayer (five times a day towards Mecca, with no set prayers) and weekly Friday prayers in a mosque which was not a sacred or separate place, but just a communal space where you could be with other (male) Muslims in an act of devotion. This involved no other rituals or 'service,' apart from, perhaps, an address by a learned Muslim. It is also a teaching space.

There was the observance of an annual fast during Ramadan and at least one visit to Mecca in your lifetime. Finally there was the payment of dues for the upkeep of the faith. That was all. Doing these five things, and a simple commitment to Allah in the initial statement of faith made you a Muslim.

Anything else beyond this, anything that came between the individual believer and his or her God, was forbidden. Anything that enchanted, stimulated or dulled the senses was banned. Any kind of powerful stimulant or symbolism that went without mediation to the human heart and soul without the control of the believer was taboo.

Hence all alcohol and other drugs were totally banned. Music, except a special drum played by women at weddings and, occasionally, unaccompanied religious singing, was banned in many parts of the Islamo-sphere. No sculptures or two-dimensional paintings were allowed. No representations in any medium which showed any living thing were allowed, for it could appeal to the viewers or listeners' emotions. Only God could make living things, not artists.

Only abstract, non-symbolic, geometrical, patterns were allowed to adorn mosques and houses. As part of this, the wonderful calligraphy woven round the Arabic characters was permitted. So the great art forms in mainstream Islam were calligraphy and architecture – the great mosques and mausoleums which are a wonder of the world. It should be remembered, however, that in certain Islamic civilisations, for example Moghul India, some of these rules were set aside, as in the beautiful miniatures.

* * *

The 'point of origin' also explains much of Islam, which is the absence of any separation between politics and religion. Mohammed was both the Pope and also Caesar, he was at the same time the religious, political and military leader. Although later there were some divisions in some of the Islamic realms between caliph, sultan and grand vizier, at the centre was the unification of power and belief.

From the first, Islam was a religion spread by conquest, a martial religion. It was immensely successful both militarily and spiritually, spreading over much of the Middle East, North Africa and most of Spain within two centuries.

From its beginning, the central task of Islam was to spread the true faith through the world. It was forbidden, as the Prophet pronounced, to force people to convert, though, through conquest or enslavement you could create the conditions where people would be eager to convert. So Islam respected and tolerated the other two monotheisms, Judaism and Christianity, which shared its Abrahamic roots. It was in some ways more tolerant than medieval Christianity. Yet it also waged war, *jihad*, on all who had abandoned Islam (apostates), on all those who believed in more than one God (polytheists), and all those who believed in none (atheists). They were to be destroyed and sent to Hell.

* * *

Just as there was no separation of religion and politics, so there was no separation of either of these from law. The *sharia* was a holy law. All of the legal code and process had been set out in the Koran and the collected sayings of Muhammad. There could be no new statutes or enactments, new departures, few legal fictions to get round earlier rigidities or adapt to new conditions. There were no professional lawyers or judges, in the sense of a particular training or formal qualification.

The process was simple, penal (and often harsh), largely concerned with morality, family disputes and crime. There were no separate jurisdictions for different parts of life (civil, criminal, ecclesiastical, commercial) and no due process involving juries or appeals. The courts did not try heresy, because heresy in the absence of much dogma did not exist. So there was nothing equivalent to the Catholic Inquisition.

There was no complex, developed, autonomous sphere of civil law to deal with economic and social disputes. In some ways this is strange since Islam, above all, was the greatest trading, merchant civilisation in the world. It controlled many of the flows of precious commodities from as far as China to Spain for three quarters of a millennium – silk, spices, porcelain, paper.

So Islam was highly sophisticated in its contractual relations, and indeed contract, that is the agreement between free and equal individuals to do something, was its central feature, making it very modern. Yet the contracts were unlike those in the West. When there was a dispute over a breach of contract in Islam, it was the intent of the contract, why it was entered into, in other words the morality, rather than the content of the contract and whether it was fulfilled, which was of most concern.

* * *

The simplicity of the highly contractual legal system, and

the hostility to all forms of group which would divide the allegiance of an individual, led to another great difference with Western law. This was the general absence of the concept of the corporation, that is a body (corpus) which consisted of a number of people who shared in its existence. Corporations are legal entities, groups of people setting up an imaginary 'body,' recognised by the state, although they were set up by individuals to promote their personal ends.

Corporations take many forms: great trading or manufacturing companies, important clubs, independent universities, trusts and charities, monasteries and churches, guilds and trade unions, independent city corporations. The idea that ordinary people can pool their resources (skills, money, labour) into something which was to their mutual benefit, formed the essence of much of the wealth, civil society, democracy and dynamism of the West. Yet this device was generally absent in the Islamosphere, since such groupings would stand between the individual and his God/Ruler.

This has remained a salient feature of Islam to this day. Islam is in many ways the most individualistic, anti-corporate, civilisation in the world. It means that the basis for modern capitalism and democracy, the innumerable institutions of civil society, are largely absent. The only forms are limited. There are quasi-trusts, *waqf*, which are for a specific purpose (the upkeep of a school or water pump for example), but very much more limited than western trusts and corporations. Or strictly religious 'brotherhoods', such as the Muslim Brotherhood, which, even in their limited form, are often considered a threat to the state/religion and banned.

* * *

Another surprise is that although originating from a merchant, trading, civilisation there is a restrictive attitude towards money. On one level Islam looks highly capitalistic well before the capitalism of the West – using widespread credit, buying and selling across vast regions, with wide and complicated trading networks. Yet Islam also banned all 'usury,' that is all money lending where interest was charged on the loan.

Hence there were no banks in Islamic civilisations until Western banks were introduced into Turkey in the nineteenth century. The idea of stocks and shares, of limited liability, of joint-venture companies, of rich people lending money at interest to others was totally banned – though ways were often found to get round part of the inhibitions as time elapsed. Nowadays there are 'Muslim' banks, and even 'Muslim' stock exchanges, through various creative fictions.

The reasons usually given for the ban on lending at interest are interesting. It was partly a puritanical instinct that richer people should not be able to sit back and profit from their wealth without taking part in the effort and risk involved in using their resources. They should not become leeches, living off the hard work of others by lending them money.

Alongside this was a limited and pre-capitalist concept of money. 'General purpose money' in capitalism has three features. It is an index of value, you know how much things cost in relation to each other. It is a token of exchange, you can use it to bring things into relation with each other. For example, I will give you a token (coin) for your oranges and you can use that token to buy someone else's apples. Finally, coins can be a store of value – you can save, freeze, congeal, value, so that the coin actually has in it the fruit of labour, time, skills, sales or whatever. It is the third attribute that is missing in Islam. A coin is just a token – it contains nothing. So if you give this token to someone else and expect them to pay you interest for it you are cheating them.

It is this limited attitude to money, combined with the absence of corporations, which partly lies behind one of the questions which many who contemplate Islamic civilisations are tempted to ask. Why was Islam, in particularly the Ottomans, finally crushed by the previously far less powerful and significant West European Christian nations?

By the tenth century, Islam was, with China, the leading scientific, military and political power on earth. There were amazing scientific thinkers, architects, doctors, traders, soldiers, historians, and creators of some of the greatest art in the world. Islam stretched over much of the central belt of Asia and provided an identity and faith to millions. It does so still, with nearly a quarter of human beings proclaiming themselves Muslim. Yet after its early glories, it faded. In military terms it remained impressive until the seventeenth century, but culturally it stopped being one of the two leading civilisations around the thirteenth century. Only a part of this can be explained by the conquest of the central Islamic lands by the Mongol invaders in the thirteenth century, for they also soon converted.

* * *

One factor which partly accounts for the relative decline of Islam lies in the system of thought, particularly the attitude to past authority and how this is expressed in education. All we need to know was revealed by the Prophet. Muhammad expressly declared that 'the worst things are those that are novelties. Every novelty is an innovation, every innovation is an error, and every error leads to Hellfire.'

Thus there was in knowledge, as in law, little to be added to the first revelation. Hence the purpose of all education was to pass on what was already known. The lower schools and even the college level *madrasahs* were usually, and increasingly, conservative. The content of the education was moralistic and literary. The aim was not to learn to think independently, to question, or to learn how to solve new problems, but rather to learn by heart what was already known and pass it on to the next generation.

The whole educational system was totally different from that which grew up in the monasteries, schools and universities of the West. There, at the university level and in the best schools, mathematics, logic and rhetoric were taught as central subjects. As in western law, there was encouragement to question, argue, find out new ways of solving problems. So the West had a Scientific Revolution. Islam, having transmitted Greek knowledge to the West, then took it little further.

The abandonment of glass manufacturing in the previously greatest glassmaking area in the world, the Middle East, was another barrier. Without mirrors, test tubes, good lenses and other glass instruments much experimental science could not emerge – and all these were absent from the thirteenth century in Islam.

Most importantly, the printing of Arabic characters, either with metal print or even as wood blocks, was banned in Islam until the eighteenth century. It was thought that mass production of books would be politically subversive (as it was in western Europe) and religiously blasphemous, in mass-producing the word for God. So the whole vast effect of printing in the West, on religion, politics, learning, concepts of time and truth, was missing. As was the influence of mechanical clocks, which again were largely absent in Islam until the nineteenth century, creating an entirely different attitude to time in western Europe and Islam.

* * *

In fact the whole technology of Islamic civilisation either failed to develop much from very early on, perhaps from twelfth or thirteenth centuries onwards. The wheel was largely abandoned, partly because camels were more effective in many environments. Waterwheels and windmills were not developed to their full potential. Although there were obviously camels, goat, sheep and some horses, compared to western Europe, animals were less common, in particular the crucial animal of China, the pig, which was considered (along with dogs) as unclean. Agricultural tools and methods became increasingly antiquated and the goats added to the deforestation and desertification. Metals and mines ran out and even the early monopoly in the trade of coffee and sugar was lost to the Western empires from the 17th century.

The vast slave labour force in Islam, and the low wages of an immiserated peasantry were among the factors, along with predatory seizures and taxes, which inhibited the building of industrial plants and the use of labour-saving devices. So Islam not only missed the Renaissance, Reformation and Scientific Revolution, but crucially the Industrial Revolution.

The flat-bottomed boats suitable for the Indian Ocean and Mediterranean were soon outclassed by the Atlantic-adapted round-bottom ships of the Western powers. Islamic armies gave up recruiting effective slave soldiers. With little metal, and with no science, the cannon and handguns of Islam became inferior to those of the West from the seventeenth century. So from the failure to take Vienna in the second siege in 1683, Islam began to falter.

From the eighteenth century, as Russia invaded from the North, the British and other Empires built up their holdings in the East, which bypassed Islam's entrepreneurial role, Islam crumbled. By 1918 the Ottomans and Arabic states were in a condition where they were subjected to a humiliating dismemberment. Having invented the nation state in the nineteenth century, the European powers decided to apply their wholly inappropriate concept of nationalism to Islamic civilisation. The chaos we see in much of the heartland of Islamic civilisation is a direct consequence.

Finally, Islam's precocious and egalitarian ethic had a fatal flaw. From the start, all male Muslims were equal. It was a modern, contractual, atomistic society. But there were three groups who by nature and birth were unequal – slaves (though they could be emancipated), women and infidels.

The increasing tendency as time passed towards a systematic downgrading of women's status – not worth an education, to be sheltered in their dress and housing from dishonour, married off young, worth half a man in law and inheritance – has been noted by many observers. This, of course, is not peculiar to Islam, but is a characteristic in various forms in most civilisations. Likewise the slavery which sustained the Islamo-sphere for centuries is widespread in traditional civilisations.

* * *

I have made numerous generalisations in this short piece to make things simple. Of course when we are dealing with a great civilisation, hundreds of millions of people, over much of the middle belt of the Earth from Western Europe to China, and over a period of nearly one and a half millennia, every generalisation can be qualified. The fact that there are well-known variations between the different religious subdivisions, most notably the Sunni, Shia and Sufi, also qualifies what one can write. There are vast variations and exceptions, as there are between the various great Islamic civilisations, Arabic, Turkic, Persian, Egyptian, Indonesian, which were often at war with each other.

Yet there does seem to be a common pattern or 'deep note' across all this huge and important Islamo-sphere. This lies in the simplicity of the message of Islam, its dramatic first steps as a conquering religion, its extreme dislike of any images or groups which will distract the believer away from the new message of the brotherhood and equality of all male believers.

As Marshall Hodgson in his *Venture of Islam* puts it, it is unwise to ask 'what went wrong with Islam,' at least in trying to understand events before the twentieth century. The Islamic civilisations followed the same trajectory as other great agrarian civilisations, including China and most of central and southern Western Europe. Up to the eighteenth century, these civilisations rose up to a plateau, then hit what Mark Elvin calls 'a high level equilibrium trap.' The laws of diminishing returns, the finite energy that can be produced through animals and plants, as well as some of the tendencies towards increasing authoritarianism and warfare, halted them. The question would perhaps better be phrased as, 'what went even better' with the one civilisation which escaped from the agrarian and authoritarian trap, a small part of north-west Europe and America.

Islam has been rightly called the 'Intermediate Civilisation.' It is intermediate in geography - between the far East and the near West. It is intermediate in ecology - between the northern and southern, in the equatorial belt around the earth. It is intermediate in history, carrying the great traditions and learning of ancient middle eastern, and particularly Greek, civilisations through to modern times. It is intermediate in role - the great merchant civilisation which carried the goods of the East to the West and vice versa. It is intermediate in its structure, combining elements of the eastern civilisations such as China, with other elements of western Europe. It forms a bridge, between East and West.

FIVE

The Euro-sphere

T HERE ARE A number of difficulties in describing the Euro-sphere concisely. As with the boundaries of China and Islam, it is difficult to know where 'Europe' is. Its borders expand and shrink depending on politics and definitions. Some people take Europe to stretch as far as the middle of Russia (the Ural Mountains) others more or less limit it, as in my school days, to Western Europe. I will here take the wider Europe, including much of Russia and all of Eastern Europe, but also extending beyond the land mass of Eur-Asia. Although I hardly deal with the East or 'Orthodox' part of Europe, I agree with Norman Davies in his magisterial book *Europe*, that we cannot separate Europe into east and west in a convincing way.

Furthermore, if we think of where Europe has shaped the language, religion, economy and politics, it stretches around the world. In particular, we need to remember the great mass of South and Middle America, conquered by the Portuguese and Spanish Empires, as well as the many former imperial territories of various European powers in Africa and Asia. Again I will not deal with any of these in any detail, but they are part of the 'Euro-sphere.'

Then there is a question of what are Europe's defining characteristics. If we take four major features – religion, race, language and social ordering – then in some ways Europe stretches as far as the East coast of India. Much of this area, outside Islamic civilisations, tends to have a majority who speak an Indo-European language, come from peoples with a common Aryan origin, and arrange the social structure into four occupational orders – the rulers, priests, the merchants and the farmers of the caste system of India, or the class/order systems of the West. Only in religion, with a mixture of Islam, Hindu, Buddhist, is India very obviously different from the Western European Christian tradition.

Another difficulty is that Europe has had such a warlike, turbulent and changing history. To generalise about Roman, medieval, early modern and modern Europe, to move from the Greek philosophers through to the later twentieth century, seems an impossible task.

Then, though Europe is no larger than China even at its largest definition, it is hugely diverse. There is no common script as in China or even great common languages. In fact there are three major language families in Europe – Roman, Germanic, Slavonic. There are huge variations in agriculture, family systems, law, and religion over a very small area. The difference between Portugal and Norway or France and Hungary or Greece and Holland is immense. So where can we locate the deep note or point of origin of this turbulent civilisation which transformed itself in various massive events such as the Renaissance, and the Scientific and Industrial revolutions?

* * *

A good starting point is the work of the French historian François

Guizot. In his *General history of civilisation in Europe: from the fall of the Roman Empire to the French Revolution* (1838), Guizot suggests that the key to much of European history lies in the half millennia when the Germanic and other invaders established themselves, from about the sixth to the twelfth centuries A.D.

In this chaotic period, there was no absolute authority or overarching system. The four powers that dominate our lives grew more or less equally and remained in tension with each other. Christianity was adopted and this is the great period when the monasteries and Church carried the burden of transmitting some of the gains of previous literate civilisation. Yet the Church could not dominate everything.

The political powers were fragmented, not only between different Germanic tribal settlement areas, but also in the new system of feudalism which has been defined as the 'dissolution of the state.' The new rulers of the small kingdoms could only hold their territories by granting their followers large tracts of land and various rights. These followers in turn did the same to their followers and so on down the chain. So that there formed diffused, delegated and balanced powers with rulers forced to bribe and listen to their followers.

Meanwhile the towns were starting to re-emerge and assert their independence and trade was growing rapidly. So cities grew up and a powerful, independent, middle-class emerged in centres of wealth and legal privileges, with people concerned mainly with the making of money – in other words a bourgeoisie. Finally, as peace was established and the new agricultural technologies, currencies, transport systems grew, the farmers prospered and a large and relatively wealthy peasantry emerged.

What Guizot suggests is that, in a game where no single player could dominate, for roughly one thousand years, Europe existed in a productive tension between the four orders of rulers, priests, townsmen and peasants. They formed temporary alliances, often two against two. Hence there was no centralised, bureaucratic civilisation but a shifting system of alliances.

It was in this dynamic situation that there emerged from about the twelfth century a distinctive, progressive, civilisation. Drawing on the Islamic thinkers who had revived Greek knowledge, extending trade, improving agriculture and military technologies, and setting up universities and schools, this civilisation emerged from a shattered chaos.

* * *

In the next four centuries between the twelfth and sixteenth, despite the huge setback of the Black Death in the middle of the fourteenth century, Europe grew ever more diverse, wealthy and knowledgeable. The flowering is in the Renaissance, starting earlier, but at its peak in the fifteenth to seventeenth centuries. Rather than just rediscovering the ancient learning, a new way of looking at the world was shaped. There is an extraordinary contrast if we examine European painting, architecture, sculpture, literature, crafts and music between the middle of the fourteenth century and the middle of the sixteenth century.

There is a new accuracy, detail, realism, understanding of the underlying laws of perspective and representation. There is a new and hopeful way of looking at the world and a belief in progress and increasing perfection. The Renaissance was not just a flowering of culture, as in ninth century Spain or twelfth century China (Sung). It was a transformation of the rules of culture; the game had changed.

The same occurred with the Scientific Revolution between the sixteenth and eighteenth centuries. The great thinkers and the technological breakthroughs of both China and Islamic civilisations were a background and provided many of the tools of thought and experiment. Yet in neither was there that transformation from the sporadic, usually slow, 'random variation and selective retention,' development of reliable knowledge to a world where it was believed that, through the use of experiments, combined with geometry and mathematics, it was possible to find out the laws of our universe. The method for speeding up discovery and new technology was instituted.

The scientific revolution was not a matter of particular discoveries; it was the invention of the method of invention. It was a new philosophy, paradigm, spirit of the age, a belief in progress. It was the pursuit of new knowledge and the desire to make use of that new knowledge to fashion things which were useful for human beings. These ranged from guns and boats to new agricultural and manufacturing methods.

This created a triangle which, when it became institutionalised, has transformed our world. At the start there was a deeper understanding of the law of physics, chemistry, optics and mathematics. This theoretical knowledge could be embedded in new and better physical objects, for example glass and clocks. These objects were then mass produced. Their availability then went back to help feed the confidence, wealth and power of those who had discovered the new theories and developed the new tools. They then developed better theories, and better tools.

This cycle or triangle, the embedding of theory into objects which then allow better understanding, is now the driving force of our planet. For example, it is behind the law which predicts that the power of computers will double every year or less under current conditions, or that our understanding of the greatest - the universe - or the smallest - sub-atomic particles – will grow exponentially.

Some may dispute whether there was anything new in all of this. But not those who really understand science. For example, the great historian of Chinese science, Joseph Needham, made a graph which shows that until about the middle of the sixteenth century Chinese technology and knowledge was on a level with, if not greater than, in the West. But it had reached a plateau and hardly grew over the next three centuries.

Meanwhile, as his graph shows, in Europe from the sixteenth century there was an increasing upward curve of knowledge in all of the sciences, what is called exponential growth, each year more and more knowledge was generated in a cumulative way. So by the nineteenth century, Western embedded knowledge in the shape of ships and guns destroyed the Chinese navies and armies. The same happened, as we have seen, with the Islamic civilisations at the same time.

Another great change was in the splitting of Europe into a Protestant North, and the Catholic south. This split occurred on the top of a previous division of Christian civilisation many hundreds of years earlier between the Catholic West and the Orthodox East. After the Protestant Reformation, no single religious leader could enforce his will on all of Western Europe. The Roman Catholic Inquisition and the Index of banned books was no longer enforceable over much of Europe. The rapid spread of printing from the middle of the fifteenth century added to this diversity of thought, the confidence in progress and the spread of new ideas.

* * *

The pace of technological, scientific, social, agricultural and other changes within the immense dynamism of Europe was to a considerable extent due to its geographical position. The Romans had looked primarily to the Mediterranean, and then the Vikings had increasingly traded and raided along the Atlantic coastline. They were starting to exploit the Atlantic-facing, deeply indented by sea and rivers, physical geography of Europe. But it was the discovery of America by Columbus in 1492, and then the rounding of the African Cape and the opening up of Asia to European powers, which changed everything. It was not just a seizing of the huge wealth of South America, or starting to open up the lands of North America, or the growing slave trade, or even the wealth from the rapidly expanding Asian empires, but something more abstract as well.

The inrush of new plants, foods, drinks and crafts, and of wider ideas of other ways of solving human problems, stimulated and drastically transformed the social and cultural life and the theoretical systems of Europe. Europe within two centuries took over from Islam as the hub of a global world of trade and exchange. Then in the following two centuries European powers would expand through their empires to conquer and seize two thirds of the lands of the world – only China, Japan and the Islamo-sphere for a while resisted successfully.

The European conquests gathered pace particularly from the middle of the nineteenth century as a result of the final transformation which gave the Euro-sphere its new power. This was the Industrial Revolution, which first put Britain half a century ahead of the rest of the world, but then was followed by Germany, France, North America and elsewhere from the middle of the nineteenth century. This is a revolution because it changed all the laws of economics and population.

It was impossible to rise above a certain threshold using just the energy of the sun through animals and human labour. There is only so much that plants and animals, and even wind and water power, could do. So that it was only when the vast reserves of coal, and later oil, the stored carbon energy of millions of years, was released through machinery and transmitted through electricity and steam, that the world shifted on its axis.

Until Japan joined this industrial club in the later nineteenth century, and then parts of eastern Asia from the 1960s, and finally China, India and elsewhere from the late twentieth century, this new bounty was a European and American monopoly. Combined with an agricultural revolution in some parts of Europe and America, this gave the western powers an immense boost which was absent elsewhere. It is only in the last generation that this divergence has ended and a great deal of economic and technological convergence has occurred.

* * *

Guizot's story of the splitting of late Roman imperial unity into the constituent parts of rulers, church, cities and peasants, a splitting which released the immense power of human creativity and continues to this day in some respects, needs one major modification.

There has always been a potential tension within European history because of the fact that in many ways, unlike all the other civilisations, Europe really has *two* points of origin not one. The earlier point of origin was the more than thousand years of Graeco-Roman civilisation which laid the foundation for later developments. Yet this first foundational point of origin was shattered and mixed up with an entirely different point of origin, that is in the nomadic Germanic warring tribes which brought down the Roman Empire, and later the waves of Slavic and Mongolian peoples.

The great civilisation of Rome (absorbing Greek ideas) had covered much of the area which many people consider to be Europe. Yet, after its collapse the roads, viaducts, cities and farms decayed. The legal and political systems of late Rome appeared to wither, even the language was replaced and new customs and technologies took over. Yet that point of origin was not entirely lost to the forces from the Germanic forests.

The story from the Renaissance in the fifteenth century onwards is also a story of the revival of that first point of origin in Rome. Whether in art, literature and learning, or what is called the 'Reception' of Roman law, that is the spreading of late Roman (Justinian) law codes and methods across most of continental Europe, Roman thought was revived.

Likewise there was a re-growth of a basically urban civilisation, where most power was in the civilised ('civis' means city) walled cities, which were surrounded by a mass of labouring, illiterate, peasants. In the East of Europe, the Orthodox belt, the peasant workers were subjected to a second serfdom. In the West, as population increased, they found themselves working ever harder with increasingly archaic tools and fewer animals.

* * *

We see from the sixteenth century the founding of a new, hybrid, civilisation. The revival of Roman imperial law, the revival of the Roman Church in the Counter-Reformation from the sixteenth century, the revival of all things Roman, including a caste-like division based on birth between the social orders. There grew up a more authoritarian family system, an educational system which was based on privileging book learning.

The success of this revival of neo-Roman imperialism, largely occurred because it was encouraged and supported by one of the four orders, namely the King and his close nobility. Late Roman imperial law treats the Emperor as divine, there is absolute power. All lower centres of power, found in Europe in the cities, local nobility, universities, local *parlements*, and even any kind of national assembly, needed to be diminished.

The King and central court achieved this re-assertion of authority partly through a device used in the late Roman Empire after it became Christian, namely through a pact between 'Caesar' and the 'Pope.' Religion and politics are re-united, with the Papal Inquisition into heresy becoming a branch of both the Church and the State, whether in Portugal, Spain or Italy, as one joint power. This alliance comes to dominate all the hitherto powerful alternatives such as the nobility, the bourgeoisie or the peasants.

Very rapidly, if we compare Europe in, say, 1600 and 1750, there grew over much of Europe a new system of large states ruled by absolutist rulers – Peter the Great in Russia, Frederick the Great in Prussia, Louis XIV in France, Carlos III of Spain.

Independent powers of all other kinds – groupings, corporations and civil society were systematically crushed.

The consequence was a loss of dynamism. The Dutch or the Italians, at the forefront of knowledge and art in the sixteenth to seventeenth, were no longer producing great and innovative breakthroughs. The Spanish, Portuguese, French and Italians were increasingly living in countries which, after influx of wealth from conquest, were either flat or declining in their economy and technologies.

Europe had hit a 'high-level equilibrium trap' in all senses and there seemed no escape from the Malthusian or Adam Smithian traps of an agrarian world. It was not dissimilar to China and the Islamo-sphere in the same period.

* * *

This reassertion of centralisation, bureaucracy, destruction of alternative sources of power in the reversion to the point of origin from Rome is important to understand because it can happen to any civilisation at any time. In Europe it re-emerged in a dramatic form in the twentieth century. First in the absolutist system of Communist Russia, then with Fascism from the 1930s in most of Europe – Spain, Portugal, Italy and Germany – abandoned the gains of an open, contested, democratic and 'civil society' civilisation.

The short-term gains in power almost led to the conquest of the world by absolutism of one form or another. Only the maintenance of democracy in the Anglo-sphere, and particularly America, saved it. So Europe has tended to oscillate between two poles or points of origin. There is authoritarian unity, as in Imperial Rome for several centuries, then the absolutist age centred on the eighteenth century and then the twentieth century between 1917 and 1945. Alternately there is a hugely diverse, multilingual, competitive, free and creative Europe which stemmed from the waves of Germanic and other invasions. Combined together, they have given us most of the great music, painting, philosophy and food which we enjoy.

SIX

The Anglo-sphere

I N S O M E W A Y S the Anglo-sphere is the easiest civilisation to understand. The term, made popular in James Bennett's book *The Anglo-sphere Challenge* (2004), refers to two areas. The core is England and the rest of the British Isles. The Anglo-sphere extends to all the areas settled by people from that country and forming the core of the white part of the British Empire in the past. This includes the United States, Canada, Australia and New Zealand and some smaller territories.

It also includes those former parts of the British Empire inhabited by large native populations but shaped by being held by Britain. This includes the first British Empire of the West Indies and the second Empire of India, Burma and parts of Africa. Thus the Anglo-sphere encompasses over a quarter of mankind and, currently, because of America, is the most powerful civilisation on Earth.

The Anglo-sphere is simple to understand for several reasons. Firstly, unlike China, Japan and Europe, but like the Islamo-sphere, it has a recent 'point of origin.' This is the Anglo-Saxon period in England, from the sixth century A.D. onwards. It is simpler than Islam because for its first thousand years, apart from a period when England held parts of France, the Anglo-sphere has been contained within one small island and not spread over the whole middle zone of the world as the Islamo-sphere did. It was a small island surrounded by a protective sea, so, like Japan, it was never destroyed by military conquest which was often the fate of countries with land borders.

It is also simple because, unlike China or the Islamo-sphere, it was never destructively conquered and temporally submerged by another civilisation. Protected by the seas, only conquered once, and that by the very similar Normans, it evolved constantly. So its deep note, and its metaphorical and actual grammar never changed dramatically.

* * *

The Anglo-sphere has many recognisable features which gave it strength and allowed it to continue as a recognisable unity across much of the world. The most obvious is the language. The core Anglo-sphere speaks an Anglo-Saxon language, though with some additions, particularly from France. The grammar and syntax have not changed much and it is now the world language. Its success was due partly because of the spread of the British Empire, especially in the early years north America, but also because many find it a flexible, pragmatic, yet poetical language. Indeed its linguistic resources are one of the reasons why the one art form in which the British really excel is literature

The land of Shakespeare, Milton and Wordsworth, of Jane Austen, the Brontes and Dickens, has produced a number of the glories of poetry, drama, novels and great children's literature. Reasons for this do not just lie in the power of the language, but in several other features of the social structure and history.

The literature from Chaucer onwards strikes us as modern

and relevant because already, six hundred years ago, England was indeed 'modern' in its social structure and mentality. So in reading the literature, people around the world recognise in the novels and plays feelings and dilemmas which they currently face.

This modernity included one of the central peculiarities of this civilisation. This is that marriage, for at least a thousand years, has been on the basis of romantic love – the strong sensation of attraction which leads into a companionate union. Most of British poetry and other literature is about love, not illicit or adulterous love as in some traditions, but about finding the loved one whom one will marry.

*   *   *

The desire to find the beloved arises from the fact that uniquely, for many hundreds of years, most young people in this civilisation left home when they were very young, at between the age of eight and twelve, in order to seek their fortune with strangers. As servants, apprentices, children at grammar schools or pages in lordly households, depending on their class, they moved from family to the wider society.

This is the crucial dynamic of the Anglo-sphere, for it broke the link between family, society and economy. It set people 'free' to compete in the market and in their social, political and mental lives. This meant that England, and later the area English culture spread over, never had a traditional 'peasant' civilisation where the economy is based on family labour and joint ownership.

The Anglo-sphere was a distinctively individualistic, contractual, society – based, from the start, on the idea that each person carried within them, like Robinson Crusoe on his island, a microcosm of the whole society. He or she was the only locus of an intersection of religion, politics, economy and society. This not only means that it is an old capitalist society, but that, through education in the wider sense, there was high mobility both social and geographical and an absence of fixed hereditary castes or classes.

From teenage years onwards, the individual lost their primary bond to their parents and siblings. Romantic love was the primary mechanism, except in a tiny set of arranged marriages amongst the very powerful, for replacing this lost emotional tie to parents with another deep relationship. The person whom one chose to share one's life and rear the next generation was closer than any other family - a lateral relationship rather than the vertical relationship of the generations found almost everywhere else in the world. Hence the obsession with love, the search for a unity of mind, heart and body. Also, hence, an explanation for the children's literature.

The reason for the fact that three quarters of the great children's writers – from Lewis Carroll and Beatrix Potter, through *Peter Pan*, *The Jungle Book*, the *Wind in the Willows*, the Pooh and Piglet stories to C.S.Lewis, J.R. Tolkien and J.K. Rowling – are from Britain, is that they lament and celebrate the lost world of childhood. Through the looking-glass, or wardrobe, or platform 8 3/4, we re-enter the world of childhood innocence which is shattered when a young child leaves home, either to live with strangers as their servant or apprentice, or in boarding schools.

* * *

If the language, literature and childhood experience are keys to the Anglo-sphere, another feature which has spread equally over the world as the core of the civilisation is law. The well-developed customary laws of the Anglo-Saxons were strengthened by the French, the Normans and Angevins, in the eleventh to thirteenth centuries and remains the law to this day. The legal system is totally different from the Roman Law systems that re-emerged on the continent from the fifteenth century. For example, English Common Law is based on different concepts of property – owned by an individual and not a family, with rights of people to dispose of their property both in life and after death as they will.

English law is based on absolute rights or liberties of the individual over their own bodies and lives. They cannot be imprisoned without proper cause and they must be quickly brought to trial. They are protected by a jury, which consists of twelve fellow citizens or subjects who stand between them and the state. An accused person cannot be convicted by the state unless a majority of these twelve are persuaded of their guilt. The jury are not to be bribed or coerced and no torture is to be used in any part of the trial.

Most of the law is administered by people who are independent of the state, local manorial officers, and particularly the unpaid local gentry acting as Justices of the Peace or magistrates. This is an ancient institution dating back over six hundred years and magistrates still process most of all criminal cases in England.

The exceptional criminal law, which protects individuals, is totally different not only from traditional Roman Law with its use of torture, absence of jurors, joining of the judicial and the police function in one individual, but even more from *sharia* law in Islam and the Chinese summary judicial system of the past.

Yet the criminal law is only a small part of English law. In the massive and complex books of law, something like four fifths is devoted to civil law and an equal proportion of the cases brought in courts in England are to do with civil law. This is above all in relation to property and economics. The immensely sophisticated property law of England formed the basis of modern capitalism with its various devices – bonds and bills, bundles of property rights, mortgages and joint-stock ventures, and above all its creative use of legal fictions.

One particularly important feature of the multi-layered bundle of rights in a resource in English Common Law, was that, uniquely, it allowed a middle category between fully private and fully public, or common, property. Much of British life has depended on restricted access to shared rights. All householders have certain carefully defined rights in the village 'commons.' All walkers have carefully defined rights to go along public paths and bridleways across private land. All members have rights in colleges, swimming pools, libraries, parks and many other amenities.

This device, at the same time public and private, means that the exclusivity of totally private property, which is highly inhibiting, is overcome. Yet the resource does not suffer the 'tragedy of the commons,' a destruction through uncontrolled use, as in the oceans, mountains and forests over much of the world. The concept of shared ownership of various kinds is a key contribution in ecology and much of social life.

* * *

The 'let's pretend' which starts a children's game or story was applied to the law. The most far-reaching legal fiction or 'let's pretend,' setting up temporary, imagined, fictitious rules of a game, was the invention and development of the Trust concept from the twelfth century.

The Trust was in turn based on an original and unique separation of English law into two almost equally powerful branches over the last eight hundred years, that is between the Common Law, the formal law of the country, and Equity, meaning fairness, which dealt with justice in the wider sense. Equity courts protected weaker groups – children, women, people who were old and forgetful, the poor who could not afford to bring a case in Common Law. Nowhere else was there such a separate system ensuring justice and protected by the most senior law figure, the Lord Chancellor. The Trust was also based on widespread trust through the society, and in turn generated a wider ethic of trust between non-related friends and partners.

The Trust was a legal fiction which set up a non-governmental body or corporation. This consisted of trustees who were given property or money by someone 'in trust,' on behalf of a purpose or person. Starting as a way of avoiding death duties in the medieval period (when the King would seize back large estates after a death and only re-grant them to the heir after a large payment), these were fictitious bodies set up by private individuals, and which could not be torn down by the State.

Increasingly they formed the basis of most of the associational culture which we call 'civil society,' the groups that exist between the individual and the state. They were recognised in law and the political authorities could not destroy them. They were totally different from the corporations which had emerged all over Europe, but which Roman Law deemed to be creations of the State, and hence could easily be dismantled. So people were able to create a multitude of 'bodies,' with assets such as a meeting-place, funds, rules, a shared purpose and other resources which could last, like a living thing, for as long as the Trustees wished.

These included economic trusts – the East India Company, the Stock Exchange, the Bank of England, the Trades Unions, the great insurance companies and thousands of others which were the driving force of capitalism and empire. They also included many other kinds of association, social, political and intellectual.

There were the political clubs which were the basis for adversarial democracy, the social clubs from the grand clubs like the Athaneum down to small working men's clubs around the country. They included the intellectual trusts like the Royal Society and the British Academy, and the Inns of Court where the lawyers were trained and met, and the Universities and Colleges of Oxford and Cambridge.

There were the religious trusts which gave shelter to the growth of the powerful nonconformist groups in England which played such a major role in every aspect of life, from anti-slavery to the great business firms – the Quakers, Baptists, Methodists. Even the Catholic Church is nowadays registered as a trust in the United Kingdom. There were the games clubs which were a factor in making the team games of Britain one of its most enduring and widespread influences.

There were the multitude of philanthropic trusts we find in Britain, America and elsewhere. It is no coincidence that many of the most important international charitable and aid agencies and organisations were started in Britain: the Boy Scouts, Girl Guides, National Trust, Oxfam, Samaritans, Royal Society for the Prevention of Cruelty to Animals (and Children and Birds), and many others. Even the former British Empire itself was envisaged as a trust, set up as an artificial entity with certain purposes. Once these purposes were fulfilled, namely the education (in the widest sense) of the conquered or assimilated peoples all over the world, the 'white man's burden' could be put down. Once people had reached the stage where they were 'adult' and able to take on the responsibilities of self-government, and manage on their own, they were free to decide to do so. Gandhi and others, as lawyers, understood this and demanded their freedom – and achieved it. So that the British Empire, amazingly, was wound up in a period of twenty years after 1945. Equally extraordinary was the fact that most of its former members decided to remain in another Trust or 'club,' known as the British Commonwealth.

The proliferation of associational groupings which stand between the individual and the state is absent in all the other civilisations we have looked at, except, in certain periods, in parts of the Euro-sphere. By weakening state power and involving people in decisions over the future of their own lives, educating them in self-rule and self-confidence, Tocqueville realised was the key to democracy itself as he saw it in England and America. Without this under-pinning of huge numbers of self-running, independent, associations and informal democracy, the formal system of ballot boxes, parliaments and political parties cannot work properly.

* * *

The presence of widespread civil society was part of the background to one of the great contributions of the Anglo-sphere, namely the idea of democracy in the sense of the government being chosen by at least a substantial part of the people and presenting itself for re-election at frequent intervals. Such democracy was invented in England and has spread over the whole Anglo-sphere and partially elsewhere. Yet it cannot exist without civil society.

Democracy was possible because Great Britain avoided the tendency towards centralisation, absolutism and over-bureaucratisation that we have seen developing in Europe from the sixteenth century and which is a feature of most civilisations. Like Europe in its first thousand years after the fall of the Roman Empire, the Anglo-Saxon and medieval period saw the balance and tension between the powers of the Crown, the Church, the middle classes in the cities and towns, and also a large and affluent farming group in the countryside, from the gentry through what were called the yeomen and husbandmen. This separation and tension between contending forces was never lost in Britain. Out of the friction and balance, represented in the warring factions in Parliament, the diverse interests were reconciled and power was never drained from the lower levels up to the centre.

There was no standing army in England because it was an island, so the rulers could not threaten their people with fear of imminent invasions across land borders and hence force them into subordination. Likewise the taxes could be used for non-military purposes, improving the infrastructure and supporting economic activities.

There was hardly any central bureaucracy because most of

the work of ruling – the law and the police, local government, the maintenance of the infrastructure of roads and bridges and buildings, was delegated downwards to cities and local government. The system was largely run by unpaid, voluntary, local labour, as in the system of the Justices of the Peace, parish and local councils and numerous organisations. A vast amount of work was done by those who felt it was their obligation as gentlemen, wealthy tradesmen, or even just local inhabitants (for example they had to take it in turn to act as constables or local police) to undertake the role of ruling and keeping the peace.

So the centralised feudalism of the medieval period in Britain, with its downward delegation of power and decisions to lower and lower levels, was applied in all fields. The cities remained free with their own liberties and courts, the local gentry had very considerable power, and every unit down to the lowest level of the parish and the manor exercised power. Hence there was no need for an armed police force, for the system was self-policing.

* * *

A particular part of the system shows how this works in terms of delegation and also reflects the peculiar family system and pattern of leaving home at an early age described above. This is the educational system. The boarding school system is the oldest continuous institution in Britain, dating back to 597 A.D. The sending of children from the middle class to boarding institutions, leading to the public schools like Eton and Winchester, and then smoothly leading into the two unique collegiate universities of Oxford and Cambridge, is to be found nowhere else in the world.

This is because the system of shifting from home to society through a 'rite of transition,' putting children outside the home into an environment where they learnt the broader skills (not just book learning) to be successful in society is unique. Through an intense and multi-level experience of friendship, self-rule and self-governing (where the youngest boys were taught to wait on senior boys, and then in turn become 'prefects' or governors in their house and school), taught them the skills to run any kind of organisation, up to the British Empire. Games and competitive sports, arts and the skills of leadership and level of the persuasion, were all part of this pattern of attempting to balance individualism with team co-operation, self-confidence with modesty, creativity with ingenuity.

* * *

Mention has been made of games and sports, and these are central not just on the playing fields, but in suggesting the central feature of this Anglo-sphere civilisation. The Anglo-sphere is a vast competitive game, with winners and losers. The games and disguised fighting for resources and status within a system with no fixed classes is everywhere. All the 'games' have rules of a simple, and usually negative kind. Do not pick up the ball in a game of football unless you are the goalkeeper. Do not call another member of Parliament a liar within the House of Commons. Do not tell a lie as a witness in a legal case. Working with a few negative rules, all of these games were part of the ceaseless struggle for 'survival of the fittest,' which is the shape of individualistic capitalism.

* * *

Much of life can be made palatable and put into perspective by the last element I shall consider – humour. Alongside capitalism, the Industrial Revolution, the language, democracy, games, civil society and the law, British humour is one of this civilisation's great gifts. It does not export perfectly, so that Americans, Australians and others often find the self-deprecating, sometimes savage, ironic (saying the opposite of what you mean close) vicious (sarcasm) humour of the British in their home island sometimes incomprehensible or unwelcome.

Yet the humour, already fully formed by the fourteenth century, as we see it in Chaucer and Shakespeare, and later leading through Oscar Wilde and Bernard Shaw to the tradition of radio and television comedy in the world, is unusual. It mostly consists of pointing to the inevitable inconsistencies, contradictions, and hypocrisies, as well as the snobbery, condescension and double standards of everyday life.

The humour attempts to resolve the tensions between the four spheres of modernity – economy, belief, politics, and society – in a way which is similar to the function of myths and rituals in tribal societies. The humour helps to lighten the inequalities of life through allowing us to laugh and make fun of power and pretension.

The humour starts in the home, is taught in the schools, is practised in that unique British institution and cradle of democracy, the 'pub' or 'public house,' and is on display every day in Parliament, in the law courts, schools, universities and boardrooms. Humour unified this civilisation as much as cricket or football.

* * *

I have concentrated on that part of the Anglo-sphere, Britain, that I know from experience and from studying my mixed Scottish, Welsh and English ancestry. Yet much of what I write could be extended, with variations, across the whole Anglo-sphere.

The original intention of much of this expansion was trade. Yet gradually it was found necessary to institute government to protect the trade. The Anglo-sphere was united by the social, economic and political rules devised originally in Britain. This is a civilisation born in Britain which, in its imperial phase, and in its belligerent wars around the world, has caused huge misery and unfairness.

Yet it is also a civilisation which provides some clues about how to maintain the balanced tension between economic, political, religious and social pressures that affect our lives. The package of competition, co-operation, relative equality in social relations including gender, combined with status striving, robust humour and imagination, all of which is shown in Shakespeare's plays with their universal appeal, suggests that it is a civilisation which still has some potential.

SEVEN

The Discord or
Harmony of Civilisations

W E ARE FACED with an unprecedented situation. The flow of people over our planet is turning from a trickle to a flood. The speed of communications of ideas, attitudes and objects is also increasing exponentially. New technologies, from weapons to medicine, from computing to consumption, are also changing at a breathtaking rate. This is just the start. The world in 2016 is hugely different from that which I inhabited twenty years ago in 1996. That in turn seems light-years away from the world of my school days in 1956. Imagine a future as this pace, of population, technology and social and political change, escalates. What will 2036 or 2056 be like?

* * *

In these brief vignettes of five of the most influential world civilisations I have tried to give a rough, preliminary, map. With this, you may be able to make more sense of the confusing intermixture and confrontations of civilisations.

Obviously the appearance of each country is mixed, and there are no 'pure' cases of civilisations. Yet I still believe that like trees or people, each civilisation has certain recognisable characteristics, which is carried on through the centuries.

Civilisations are persistent and tough and can last for many centuries, even though they are constantly evolving and changing, like a language or a growing tree. Much of their character is laid down in the form of a germ or seed very early, and then this expands and incorporates new elements, but the structure remains largely unchanged. The China of 2022 B.C. or the Islam of 700 A.D. or the England of the same date can still be seen in many of its aspects to this day.

One way to envisage each of them is through the metaphor of trees. If we think of civilisations thus, and choose a tree for each civilisation, then the five civilisations can be seen as following.

China is like the national tree, the gingko. It is a 'living fossil,' immensely tough having survived many thousands of years since the age of the dinosaurs. It has an extremely simple leaf structure, but very powerful and tenacious propagating system. It is a mixture of very old and very new features. It is a miracle of nature, and its ancient and durable character well represents China.

In essence, China is a simple structure, despite its vast size. It has two main constituents. One is that everything is relational, structural, each segment consists of a relation between A and B, as with Yin and Yang. So it is infinitely extensible and practically indestructible, like a worm. The second feature is that whenever it reforms itself after the periodic massive upheavals of invasion or revolution, it returns to the highly centralised, hierarchical, based-on-meritocratic-training which the Qin Emperor instigated. This unites every person through links up to the top, and through a shared written language and Han identity, it has a sense of imagined community over a vast area.

* * *

The Japanese are like the bamboo (which is in fact a form of grass, just as a gingko is a form of fern). Again, very strong and enduring, bending with the wind but almost impossible to break. Part of the reasons for its success is again its system of propagation – through rhizomes or roots that form under the ground so that each new bamboo sprouts from another root, forming an intertwined mass, like Japanese society.

Japan is even simpler in its basic structure than China, and indeed can be said, like the fermented bean shoots in *natto*, to have no real structure at all. It is again all about relations, two hands clapping and the sound they produce, the merging of opposites, the downplaying of the individual. It is largely undifferentiated mass, both unequal in each relation, yet relatively equal in its absence of fixed castes and classes. There are no hard separations. This world and any other world overlap and merge, the economy and polity and ideology and society are undifferentiated at a deep level. It is neither pre-modern, post-modern, or modern at all, but unique as a civilisation. Again it has a strong sense of common identity and imagined community and a great ability to withstand external shocks.

* * *

The Islamo-sphere can be represented by one of its most characteristic trees, the date palm. It is heavily defended by spiky branches which protect it from marauders. It provides a delicious and vital form of nourishment (edible dates) for large numbers of people. The tree probably originated in the Iraq region and there is evidence of its cultivation and use over eight thousand years ago.

The Islamo-sphere was born in the Prophet's life in the early seventh century in the form of a great simplification of life and the clearing away of older structures. In essence, therefore, it was and is straightforward. All male, free, Muslims are equal. All believers owe their overriding allegiance to Allah. All distractions from this allegiance should be avoided. Humans are naturally good and can ascend, through faith, to Heaven. There is a fusion of politics and religion. The original writings and sayings are still entirely relevant and enshrined in the law and teaching. Change is dangerous, unbelievers are damned unless they convert, though Jews and Christians are to be tolerated.

This is not a relational or structural civilisation like China or Jan, for it is not in other humans that a person is fulfilled or completed, but in Allah. It is thus a highly individualistic, contractual, fluid world with one centre - Allah. Again it can survive shocks and pressures and spreads remarkable because of the strength and simplicity of its central vision.

* * *

The Euro-sphere can be represented by one of the most widespread of trees which flourishes both in the Mediterranean and further north, the sweet or Spanish chestnut. Prickly and menacing on the outside, once it is opened it is filled with nutritious nuts which are known as the 'bread of the poor.'

The Euro-sphere stretches from western Russia, through central and western Europe as far as South America. It is more complex than the other civilisations for it has two deep notes or points of origin. It is two streams joined and constantly in tension with each other. One is derived from Greece, through the medieval feudalism of the nearly millennium after the fall of Rome, culminating in the Italian city states and the Renaissance, and surviving to this day in democratic movements which have kept the medieval separation of the four powers of ideology, wealth, power and society.

The other stream is from ancient absolutisms of early Empires, through late Roman imperialism, by way of a revival of Roman Law and the pact between the Christian Church and the Rulers. This strand is centralised, deeply hierarchical, caste-like, mixing religion and politics, tending towards totalitarianism. These two streams are dominant in different periods.

* * *

The Anglo-sphere can be represented by the British national tree, the oak. Very long-living, very tough, used in cathedrals and the ships that kept England free, but also allowed the predation on others and the building up of the largest Empire in history. Its complex long-lived specimens, tell a story of an old and continuous development, sometimes going back over a thousand years.

This system started on a small peripheral island off Europe, derived from the Anglo-Saxons. It would not be of interest if it had not been that by chance it spread through Empire and the force of industrialisation. As a consequence it laid down much of the dominant language, laws, political system and economic organisation of the modern world.

It is a system which was early 'modern' in the sense of

destroying all solidary groupings, the family, castes, all birth-given and usually dominating institutions. The individual holds the whole civilisation within him or her self and is the only intersection of economy, society, polity and ideology. It is a civilisation noted for its loneliness, aggression philistinism and duplicity. Yet it can also show tolerance, the ability to absorb, a respect for rights and an attachment to humour and playfulness.

* * *

So we have these customary arrangements or assemblages of features, which each has its own distinctive 'deep note,' yet also influences others all the time, especially over the last half millennium.

As could be expected, each answer to the question of how to lead a reasonable and meaningful life brings its members great benefits, but also difficulties. The civilisations cannot be merged, for then, like mixing colours, we will just end up with a dull brown.

Returning to trees, there is no point in trying to force one tree to be another. What needs to happen is to allow them to coexist. Yet if one becomes diseased and weak, or becomes too strong and overshadows the others, the minimalist forester may need to bind up, or prop it up a bit, or cut-off an offending branch that is severely damaging another tree. Yet basically it is left alone to be the tree it is. So the world as a lightly managed forest is a reasonable model of coexistence.

I have watched this situation of co-existence in my garden. I have let many trees sprout and grow up and they do not attack each other, even if they sometimes have to bend to catch the light. They coexist. Only particularly rapid and thorny plants, blackberries, do I contain and root out when they spread too far and fast – though even they, the heretics and dissenters of my garden, have their value in producing rich berries.

In principle, although the structures I have described are hugely different, there is no reason why the five civilisations cannot coexist like trees in my garden, once they recognise and understand each other's strengths and weaknesses.

The tallest and the broadest will change from time to time, new saplings will thrive and perhaps some old trees will shrink and even die, as some of my old apple trees are now doing. But the forest continues peacefully and provides the best possible mix, a place for the birds to nest, the hedgehogs to roam, the butterflies and bees, even slugs and snails.

Some will say that this is a romantic vision. That 'history' shows that we are vicious predators. But 'history' is largely still assumed to be Western history. Chinese and Japanese history tells us different things. We find long periods, hundreds of years, of peace and reasonable prosperity. Even if we accept that the past, particularly of Europe, has been characterised by vicious predation, we also know that unless we do follow the trees, we will all shortly be dead. The self-fulfilling philosophy of the 'clash of civilisations' will destroy us all.

* * *

A second metaphor is also useful because it helps us to think about how we can remain different, with our own identities, yet also live together, stressing our commonality and friendship. The metaphor of harmony, which I picture as musical harmony, where though different instruments or voices maintain their own melodies, yet all of them fit together into something tuneful and mutually enriching, seems a good one for this endeavour.

The essence of harmony is that there is a tension between separate elements, which maintain their difference and identity, yet work together. What keeps the unity are the two rules on which all players must be agreed – otherwise there is discord. One is the spacing between the instruments on an agreed vertical scale, so they have to play on that scale. Playing or singing off the scale is discordant. The second is in terms of beat, tempo, so that the players come in at the right moment and for the right duration.

Once these two rules are agreed, it just needs a conductor to lead them and ensure that anyone who does not abide by these rules is led back into agreement. A minimal, 'night watchman conductor' will have the power delegated to him or her to sanction or even expel a member after due process.

With these two 'rules' in place, the tones and sounds of each civilisation may be very different and indeed it is the very difference which makes for the richness. A cello will not become a trumpet, but nevertheless they need not compete or be at war with each other. They blend their voices.

Societies are and have long been based on this idea of harmony, for example in the caste system where each caste plays its part, or in the division of labour and class in capitalist societies. So there are no *a priori* grounds for believing that higher level entities, that is a number of civilisations within one world, cannot do this.

* * *

It is not conceivable that we will be able to eradicate tensions and misunderstandings. Even between people who love each other and have come to understand the other over many years, there are moments of anger and misunderstanding. How much more so between the huge confusion of fast amalgamating civilisations.

Yet we can mitigate some of the effects through understanding each other a little better and even learning to love each other a little, or at least to admire and be amused by each other. At least that is my hope, and one of the main reasons why I have tried to understand these five civilisations. Fear and ignorance, at least, can be decreased, and a world in which we are going to have to live for centuries to come in a set of relations which are unprecedented may be made a little more harmonious.

As I look out on my December garden in the Cambridgeshire fens at the winter-flowering honeysuckle and the bare trees, things look less than hopeful. Yet I know that the spring and summer will bring everything back to life and the numerous, largely untended shrubs and fruit trees and numerous majestic chestnuts and limes will bring shade and peace.

ALAN MACFARLANE

How We
Understand the World

THIS BOOK IS part of a series of short letters written to young friends. Encouraged by the reception of my *Letters to Lily* (2005), I decided to write a set of letters to her younger sister – *Reflections for Rosa*. I was then asked by other friends to write short books for their children.

In each I try to explore some aspect of 'How We Understand the World,' based on my experience as an anthropologist and historian at Cambridge University. I have tried to put into simple words what I have learnt about discovery, creativity and methods to understand our complex world.

EXPLORE THE SERIES

CAM RIVERS
PUBLISHING

Image on front cover is an adaptation of The Tower of Babel by Pieter Bruegel the Elder, available in the public domain.